THE GOOD DINOSAUR

Ages 4–5

Numbers and Counting

LEARNING WORKBOOK

Scholastic Children's Books
Euston House,
24 Eversholt Street,
London NW1 1DB, UK

A division of Scholastic Ltd
London ~ New York ~ Toronto ~ Sydney ~ Auckland
Mexico City ~ New Delhi ~ Hong Kong

Published in the UK by Scholastic Ltd, 2016.

ISBN 978 1407 16491 5

Printed in China

2 4 6 8 10 9 7 5 3 1

www.scholastic.co.uk

Welcome to the Disney Learning Programme!

Children learn best when they are having fun! The **Disney Learning Workbooks** are an engaging way for your child to develop their number and counting skills, along with fun characters from the wonderful world of Disney.

The **Disney Learning Workbooks** are carefully levelled to present new challenges to developing learners. Designed to support the Early Years Foundation Stage Profile for Numeracy, this title offers your child the opportunity to practise skills learned at school and to consolidate their learning in a relaxed home setting with support from you. With interactive stickers, games and craft activities, your child will have fun learning about numbers and counting.

In this book, your child will practise their numeracy skills and reinforce their understanding of the numbers 1 to 20. There are many activities to help your child to: practise counting objects, match numerals to the written number, use number lines, order the numbers to 10 and recognise the numbers up to 20.

Throughout the book you will also find 'Let's Read' stories featuring the characters from the Disney film **The Good Dinosaur** for you to enjoy sharing with your child. Reading for pleasure and enjoying books together is a fundamental part of learning. Keep sessions fun and short. Your child may wish to work independently on some of the activities or you may enjoy doing them together – either way is fine.

Have fun with the Disney Learning programme!

Developed in conjunction with Charlotte Raby, Educational Consultant

Learning to count is fun. When you know the numbers, you can count anything. When Arlo was just an egg, he didn't know about counting. Now he counts sweetcorn on the family farm and fireflies in the dark night sky.

In this book you will learn how to count to 20!

Number Line

You will find out how to use a number line. There are number lines on lots of the pages of the book to help you remember the order of the numbers. Use a number line if you ever get stuck.

Number Line

0 1 2 3 4 5 6 7 8 9 10

Here are some easy ways to count:

You can use a rhyme to help you to remember the numbers 1 to 10.

1, **2** Arlo and you,

3, **4** play some more,

5, **6** pick up sticks,

7, **8** lay them straight,

9, **10** begin again!

Practise saying the rhyme again all by yourself!

Fingers
Spot has ten fingers. These are very useful for counting. Count on your fingers. They are always there to help you!

Answers
If you need to check your answers, turn to page 47.

11 12 13 14 15 16 17 18 19 20

Henry and Ida lived at the base of Clawtooth Mountain. The two Apatosauruses took good care of their farm. Soon they would have a family.

One day, while Henry was working in the fields, Ida called out, "It's time!"

Henry and Ida eagerly watched as their three eggs began to hatch. The first was a healthy girl named Libby. The second was a strong boy named Buck. But inside the biggest egg was a tiny dinosaur too afraid to come out.

"Hello, Arlo," said Poppa proudly.

Let's count to 5. Say the numbers out loud.

1 2 3 4 5

Now trace the dots and write the numbers.

Can you help Momma count the hatched eggs?

Count the eggs and stick the right number sticker in each box.

Let's count to 10. Say the numbers out loud.

1 2 3 4 5
6 7 8 9 10

Now trace the dots and write the numbers.

Let's Order Numbers to 10

Let's write the numbers 1 to 10 in order.

Write the number beneath each picture.

A

0 1 2 3 4 5 6 7 8 9 10

B

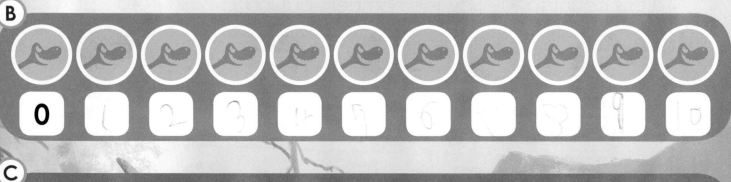

0 1 2 3 4 5 6 7 8 9 10

C

0 1 2 3 4 5 6 7 8 9 10

Can you fill in the missing numbers
on these number lines?

D
0 1 2 3 4 5 6 7 8 9 10

E
0 1 2 3 4 5 6 7 8 9 10

F
0 1 2 3 4 5 6 7 8 9 10

G
0 1 2 3 4 5 6 7 8 9 10

You can write any number
as a word or a numeral.

So the number one can be written as...

one or **1**

Find the stickers that match the number.

One 1

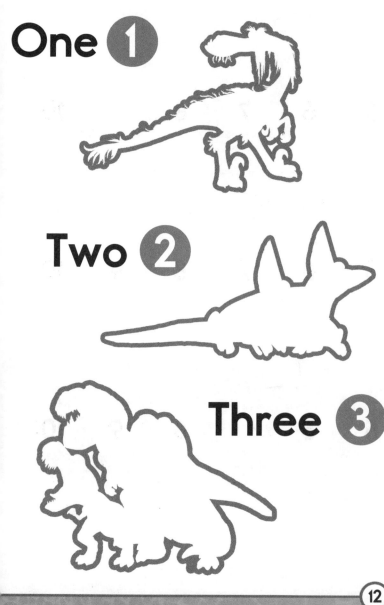

Two 2

Three 3

Four 4

Five 5

Six 6

Seven 7

Eight 8

Nine 9

Ten 10

Buck is working hard piling logs on the farm. He needs five piles of logs in each field.

Make sure each field has 5 log piles.
Use your stickers to add the right number.

1

Buck has made
4 log piles.

2

Buck has made
3 log piles.

3

Buck has made
2 log piles.

4

Buck has made
5 log piles.

5

Buck has made
1 log pile.

Use the number line to help you count the Raptors.

0 1 2 3 4 5 6 7 8 9 10

Number Line

Write how many in each box.

Let's Learn Ordinal Numbers

There is another way of saying numbers.

We can say 1st, 2nd, 3rd, 4th and 5th.

Who's won the race?

Draw a line from each runner to the correct rosette.

Let's Match Amounts to Numerals

Poppa has asked Arlo to put the cluckers into pens, but he has lost count. Each pen contains some cluckers. Count how many there are and then match the correct number to each pen.

(10) (1) (5) (7) (4) (2)

Draw a line from the pens to the numbers.

Spot is wrestling with a giant insect. Count the insects in each box, then answer the question.

A There are 4 insects in the sky.

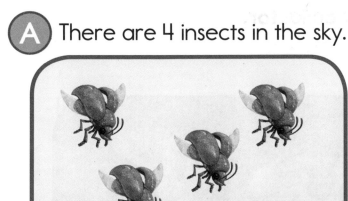

1 insect flies away.
How many are left? 4

B There are 5 insects in the sky.

1 insect flies away.
How many are left?

C There are 7 insects in the sky.

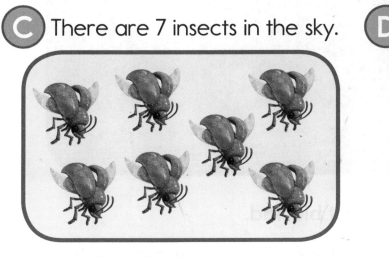

1 insect flies away.
How many are left? 7

D There are 2 insects in the sky.

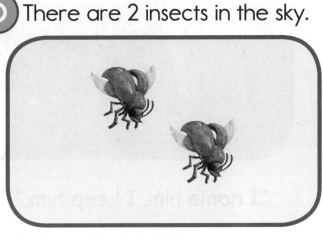

1 insect flies away.
How many are left? 2

Forrest Woodbush the Styracosaurus collected creatures to protect him. He wanted to add Arlo's critter to his collection.

"He's with me," said Arlo.

"What's his name?" said the pet collector.

"I-I don't know," said Arlo.

"I name him, I keep him," Forrest blurted.

He and Arlo began calling out names. The critter didn't respond. But when Arlo shouted, "Spot!" the critter ran to him.

Forrest told Arlo that Spot would keep him safe.

Arlo and Spot continued along the river.

Spot sniffed out a gopher and chased it into a hole. Spot blew into the hole. The gopher popped up out of another hole!

Then Arlo blew into a hole, and a bunch of gophers popped out of the ground. Arlo and Spot laughed, until one of the gophers bit Arlo, and he fell into a lake. Shocked by the cold water, Arlo struggled to stay afloat. But when Spot jumped in and began doggy paddling, Arlo mimicked him.

Soon Arlo was swimming, too!

Forrest Woodbush's protective creatures keep toppling off and some have even run away.

He needs 10 creatures on his horns.

A

How many more creatures make 10?

7

Look at the two pictures below and then
add the correct number of creatures using your stickers.

B

How many more
creatures make 10?

Now you can count to 10 let's count to 20.
Say the numbers out loud.

11 12 13 14 15
16 17 18 19 20

Now trace the dots and write the numbers from 11 to 20.

Number Line

0 1 2 3 4 5 6 7 8 9 10

Count the number of footprints, then write it in the box.

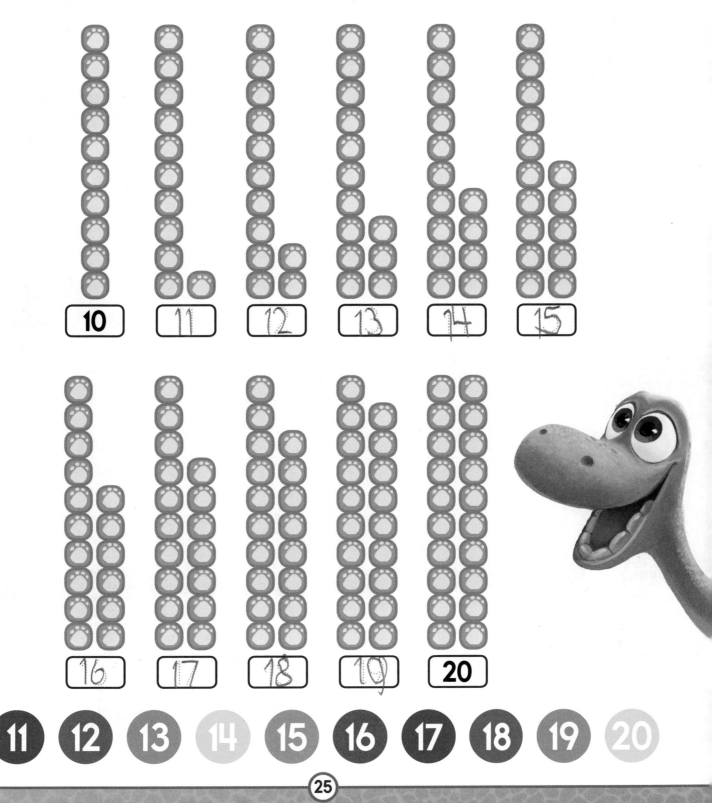

10 11 12 13 14 15

16 17 18 19 20

11 12 13 14 15 16 17 18 19 20

Let's Make Dino Feet

Arlo has great big dinosaur feet.
They take him on a big adventure.
Try making your own dino feet!

You will need:

- 2 empty tissue boxes
- 2 paints (blue and yellow)
- 1 piece of white paper
- 1 glue stick
- 1 pair of scissors

Crafts are more fun with family. Ask a grown-up to help.

What to do:

1. Mix the 2 paints to make green.

2. Paint the 2 tissue boxes green, and then let them dry.

3. Draw 6 'toes' for Arlo's claws on the white paper and cut them out.

4. Use the glue to stick 3 toes on each tissue box.

5. Put your feet on and stomp like a dinosaur!

It's easy to make your own dino world. Remember your numbers as you count and make.

You will need:

- 1 clean jam jar
- 1 large leaf or piece of fabric
- 1 elastic band or piece of string
- 2 or 3 small dinosaur toys
- 20 pebbles or small stones
- Some sand or moss

Count the items carefully to make sure you have everything ready!

What to do:

1. Place the sand, moss or pebbles in the bottom of the jam jar.

2. Count the dinosaurs as you place them carefully inside the jar. Make sure they can stand up!

3. Lay the leaf or fabric over the jam jar lid.

4. Carefully, secure the leaf in place by putting the elastic band over it or by tying the string around the leaf.

Arlo's world is full of dinosaurs and critters.
Count them all.

How many can you see?

Add a number sticker in the box.

Raptors **[3]**   Butterflies **[2]**

Pterodactyls **[5]**   Big-eared Foxes **[7]**

Flying Bugs **[2]**   T.rexes [ ]

Let's Complete a Number Line

Now you know the numbers 1 to 20.

Let's write them in order.

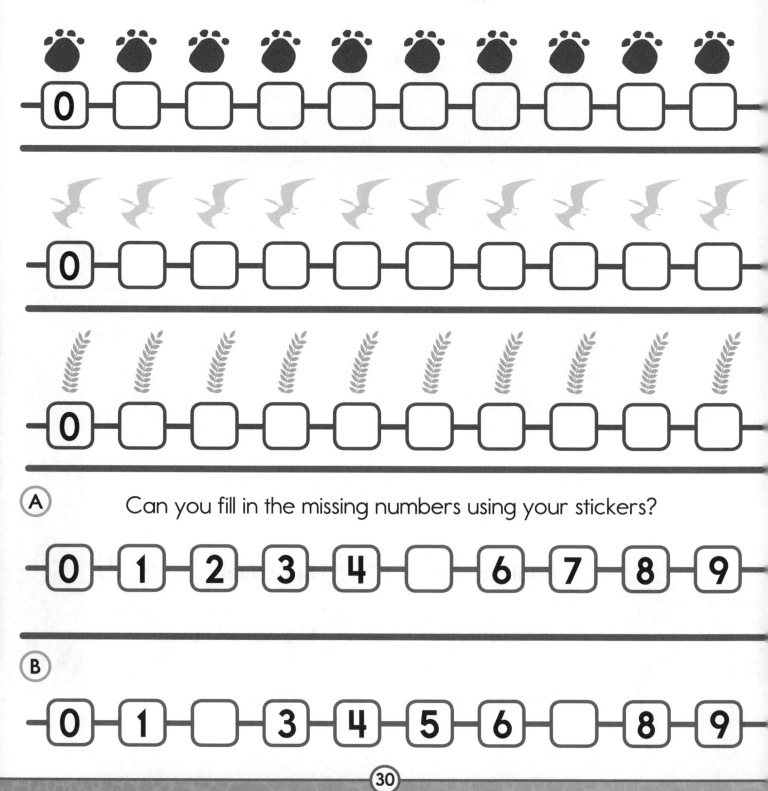

A Can you fill in the missing numbers using your stickers?

0 1 2 3 4 ☐ 6 7 8 9

B

0 1 ☐ 3 4 5 6 ☐ 8 9

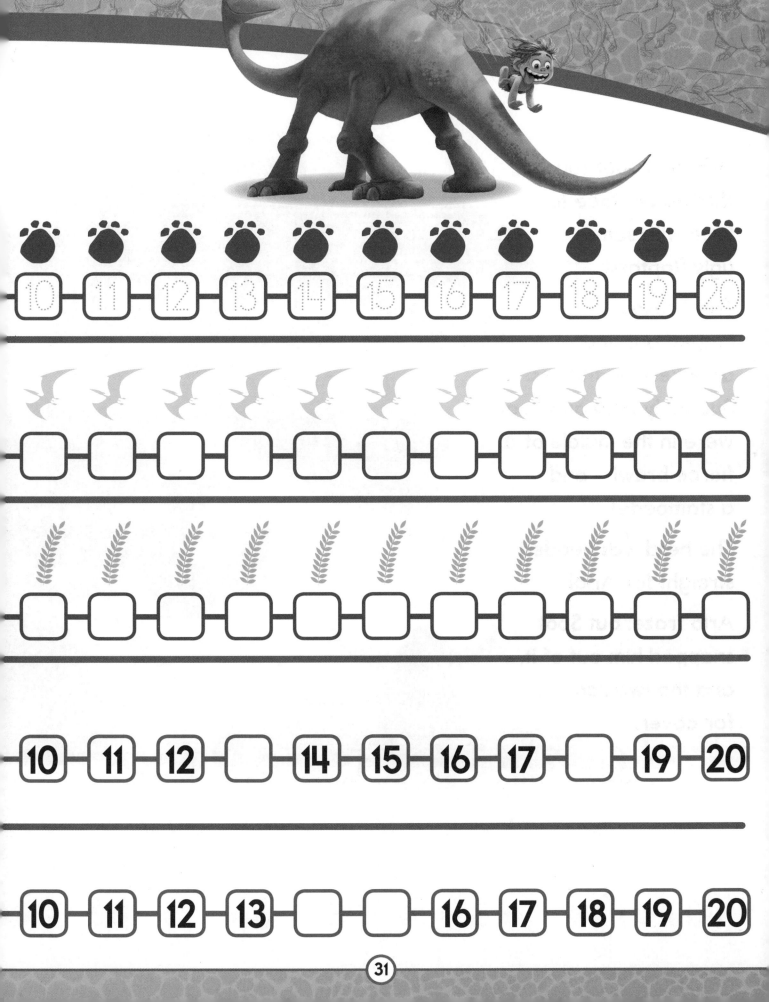

10 11 12 13 14 15 16 17 18 19 20

| 10 | 11 | 12 | | 14 | 15 | 16 | 17 | | 19 | 20 |

| 10 | 11 | 12 | 13 | | | 16 | 17 | 18 | 19 | 20 |

Arlo and Spot found themselves face to face with some ugly Raptors!

The T.rexes leaped out and attacked the thieves. Suddenly Arlo and Spot were in the middle of a fierce brawl – and a stampede!

The herd was headed straight for Arlo!

Arlo froze, but Spot snapped him out of it, and the two ran for cover.

When the Raptors pinned Butch to the ground, he called for Arlo's help. Without thinking, Arlo head butted the rustler off of him. With the tide turned, the T.rexes chased them away.

Arlo joined the T.rexes in a triumphant roar.

Let's Find One More or Less

Can you find the numbers which are one more or one less?

Number Line

0 1 2 3 (4) 5 6 7 8 9 10

4 is one less than 5.

Number Line

0 1 2 3 4 5 (6) 7 8 9 10

6 is one more than 5.

Now it's your turn.

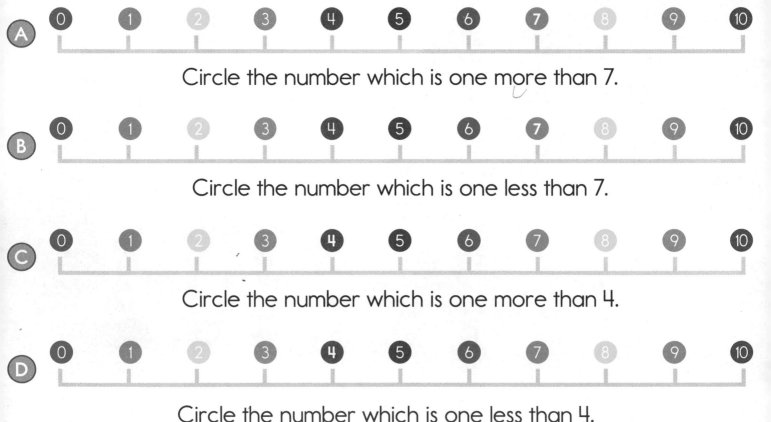

(A) 0 1 2 3 4 5 6 7 8 9 10

Circle the number which is one more than 7.

(B) 0 1 2 3 4 5 6 7 8 9 10

Circle the number which is one less than 7.

(C) 0 1 2 3 4 5 6 7 8 9 10

Circle the number which is one more than 4.

(D) 0 1 2 3 4 5 6 7 8 9 10

Circle the number which is one less than 4.

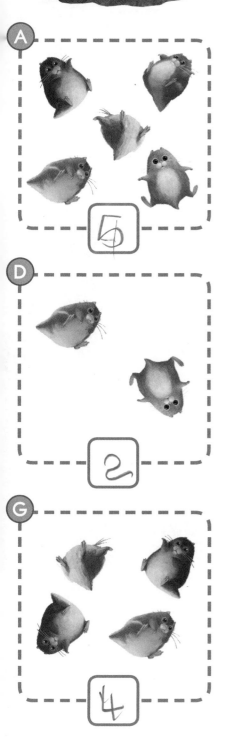

Count the Gophers

Write how many there are in each box.

Which box has the most gophers?

A 5

B 3

C 6

D 2

E 7

F 1

G 4

H 5

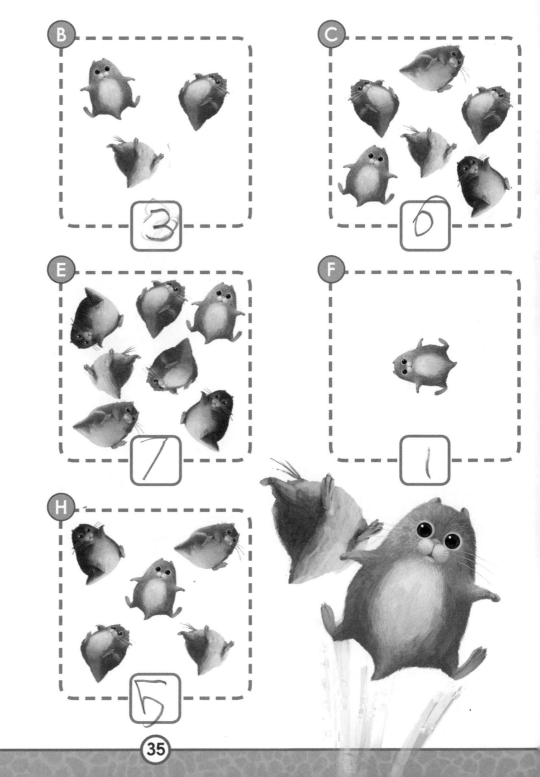

Count the footprints on the rock and
write the number in the box.

Tick the rock that has the most footprints.

A

B

C

D

Arlo is following the numbers to get home,
but some of the numbers have gone missing.

Stick the numbers in the right place,
so Arlo can get home.

1 2 ◯ 5 4

6

8 ◯

11 ◯ 13

9

◯ 15 14

17 ◯

20

18 ◯

The River Game

Find out how to play the River Game.

First, make sure you have 2, 3 or 4 players.

Ask an adult to help with this.

You will need:

- A piece of card
- Scissors
- Counter stickers
- A dice

How to set up the game:

1. Find the counter stickers on the sticker spread and stick them onto the card.

2. Cut round the stickers to create four player counters.

3. Each player chooses a counter and places it on **START**.

4. Decide which player will go first.

Let's play the River Game!

1. Player rolls the dice and moves his or her game piece the number of spaces shown on the dice.

2. If the player lands on a special space, they must follow the instructions, then end their turn.

3. The next player takes their turn.

4. The first player to reach **FINISH** is the winner.

The River Game

Can you follow the river home?

START

1

2 — Forrest Woodbush wants to collect you! **Miss a turn.**

3

4

5

6

7 — Waterfall! **Go back 3 spaces.**

8

9

10 — You help a T.rex out! **Go forward 2 spaces.**

14 Raptor panic! **Run back 5 spaces!**

15

16 Hitch a ride on a giant bug! **Go forward 3 spaces.**

12

13

17

11

18 You've nearly made it!

20

19

FINISH

Here Are All The Things I Can Do!

Stick a dinosaur footprint next to each thing that you can do.

I can...

Remember a useful counting rhyme ◯

Write the numbers 1 – 10 ◯

Use my fingers to count ◯

Order numbers to 10 ◯

Recognise and count the numbers 1 – 5 ◯

Recognise number words from one to ten ◯

Write the numbers 1 – 5 ◯

Use a number line to 10 ◯

Recognise and count the numbers 1 – 10 ◯

Make the number 5 by adding more ◯

Learn ordinal numbers from 1st to 5th ⬤

Order numbers to 20 ⬤

Match amounts to numerals ⬤

Use a number line to 20 ⬤

Count one less ⬤

Use a number line to add one more ⬤

Make 10 by adding more ⬤

Use a number line to find one less ⬤

Recognise and count the numbers 1 – 20 ⬤

Compare numbers and tick the most ⬤

Write the numbers 1 – 20 ⬤

Count spots on a dice, then move my counter to play a game ⬤

Follow counting instructions in a craft activity ⬤

Numbers are everywhere!

We use numbers constantly. The best way for your child to learn about numbers is for them to see them being used every day. Help your child to notice the numbers in the environment: on road signs, house numbers, in shops and in games. Involve your child in tasks where they have to count, such as bringing cutlery to the table. The more your child uses numbers themselves, the more they will enjoy learning about them.

Counting rhymes

It is much easier to learn when it's fun, and a great way to do this is to chant or sing counting rhymes. Sing songs such as 'Ten green bottles', 'Five little ducks went swimming one day', 'Five little monkeys jumping on the bed', and '1, 2, 3, 4, 5, once I caught a fish alive'. These songs all teach counting in a fun, memorable way.

The shopping game

Children are interested in what you do, so involve them in shopping. Ask them to help you write lists. They can write the number of each item that you need. The shopping game is a fun game to play to increase your child's memory and practise their counting. You start the game by saying: 'I went to the shop and bought 1 banana,' the next person has to remember the previous item and add 2 of another item. Keep on counting and adding items. Can you get to 10 items or more?

Recipes

Simple recipes are a fantastic way to involve your child in counting, and they have a delicious end result! Ask your child to help you weigh ingredients. Read the recipe together and point out the numbers to your child. Ask them to get you ingredients and utensils. Get them to help you set the timer and encourage them to watch the timer, so they can see the numbers count down.

More or less?

Once your child has a good understanding of number order and can count confidently to 10, you can start to talk about the concept of more or less. Start with objects; make two piles of toys and ask your child to tell you which pile has more objects in it. They may well do this by size of the objects, so ask them to count the number.

Number lines

Number lines help children see the relationship between numbers. Use a number line to help your child see where the numbers are in relationship to each other. Explain that the further a number is to the right, the more (or greater) it is. Play games with the number line. Hop along the number line in patterns of 2 or 3. Choose two numbers and count how many hops of 1 there are between them. Put a number line up on your fridge so that your child can see the numbers in order everyday!

Dice games

Playing games with dice is a great way to recognise the numbers 1-6. Any board game that involves moving spaces each time you throw the dice will strengthen your child's counting skills. If you play games with two dice, your child will start to try simple addition.

Page 9

2 4 3 5

Page 11

D. 5, E. 9, F. 2, G. 4 & 7.

Page 15

9, 7, 6, 4, 2, 3.

Pages 16-17

Page 18

Page 19

A. 3

B. 4

C. 6

D. 1

Pages 22-23

A. 3 B. 5

Pages 28-29

Raptors	3	Butterflies	2
Pterodactyls	5	Big-eared foxes	6
Flying bugs	7	T.rexes	2

Pages 30-31

A. 5, 13, 18.

B. 2, 7, 14, 15.

Page 34

A. 8, B. 6, C. 5, D. 3.

Page 35

A. 5, B. 3, C. 6, D. 2

E. 7, F. 1, G. 4, H. 5

Box E has the most with 7.

Page 36

A. 18, B. 16, C. 20, D. 14

Rock C has the most prints.

Page 37

Add stickers 3, 7, 10, 12, 16, 19.

CONGRATULATIONS!

_____

(Name)

has completed the Disney Learning Workbook:

NUMBERS AND COUNTING

Presented on

_____

(Date)

_____

(Parent's signature)